The Guards

Selected Poems, 1960 - 2015

by

Malcolm McCollum

YouArePerfectPress

Acknowledgments

Black English - Janus and SCTH 5/2, October, 1973
Western Haiku - Janus and SCTH 3/3, January, 1972
Round Lake - Almagre, 2002/Poetry While You Wait, 2009
Muscular Christians - Almagre, 2000
The Great Nagurski's Blocking Guard - The Eleventh Muse, Fall 1987
Cousins - The Eleventh Muse 14/1, Spring/Summer 1997
The Three Geese Dance - The Poet Said What? April, 2000
In the Gray Evening Which May Rain - Poetry While You
The Hawk Moth - Poetry While You Wait, April, 2010
The Buddha's Funeral - Prairie Smoke (Pueblo Poetry
Blue Light - Blue Light Review #9, Winter 87/88
We All Want to Change the World - Pudding 49, 1995
Botticelli's Aphrodite - Voice, Verse and Vision, 2010

ISBN: 978-0-9844139-4-2

Library of Congress Control Number: 2016935433

YouArePerfect Press
Lancaster, New Hampshire

For Thelonika, Jason, Lestat, Magdalena,
Zeppelin, and Emberleigh

Preface

I wrote this poem early in the 1970's:

The Guards

The Chinese temple dogs bug
their pottery eyes and hang
their glazed eyeteeth over
their lower lips.

They squat with power
at the temple's mouth,
fierce and funny.

Say only what you know,
not often, and quit.

That sums up my artistic taste and creed, if I have either. I listen to Mozart rather than Beethoven, Satie, rather than Wagner. I read a lot more Robert Frost than I do Whitman, more Vonnegut than Wolfe. I just don't cotton to the big picture.

Somewhere I learned that one of my favorite poets, Thomas Hardy, wrote poems most of his life and never tried to publish them, just finished them up and slipped them into a drawer. After he'd gained success as a novelist and was getting old, he started pulling them out of the drawer, and set about getting them published to the world.

I've done the same, not because I was a successful novelist or writer of any kind, but because writing poetry was one of the things I did, and because I was too busy doing other things to spend the time it takes to get published.

So I've opened the drawer and pawed through the mess therein, and these are the poems written over most of my lifetime I think worth keeping alive.

I'd guess that out of every hundred pages of poems I've read, I might have found one that spoke to me. Out of every thousand pages, maybe one or two has spoken to me so clearly about something I cared for that I've copied it down so's to remember it. Reading poems is like looking for love - unpredictable, dangerous, and just about as individual as you can get.

I've organized these babies into decades, but we all know that whatever it is that moves within history or societies doesn't operate on our clocks, and that, say, the "60s" didn't really get going until about 1963, or end in 1970. Just a little set of drawers for you readers. And I hope you find a poem or two in one drawer or another that speaks to you truly enough that you'll want to remember it and pass it on.

The Sixties

The Seventies

The Eighties

The Nineties

The New Millenium

The Sixties

Death of Lenny Bruce

I am driving home.
Trees are becoming distinct.
Hog futures will be high,
Cloud ceilings low today.
I have one cigarette,
But somewhere I seem
To have thrown my last match
Away.

Cousins

They know the price of everything,
Hatchet to rake, handsaw to lantern,
Pflueger reel to Peters shell.
Prices go up through the years.
They always keep track.

So they know what it costs
To chop, to burn a pile of leaves,
To let the blade drift through a plank
Welling yellow sawdust,
To light a cold barn, to kill.

All summer long, the gas heater burns
Above the store where they sit at noon.
Where we sit, much obliged
By blood to stifle and ache
From nothing to say.

Flames waver blue behind the isinglass.
They know the price of gas, too,
But the world gets colder through the years.
I know that now, but knowing it,
I still could not wait to run away.

Fish Dancer

Where the shore bends, there a pike lies,
a walleye once, but birds ate his eyes
and ladybugs nest in the sockets now.

Once after a storm I walked the beach,
dancing away from the waves' running reach -
a deadly moonlit minstrel show.

A comfort to think myself a prize
of some dark cherishing deep below,
whatever a pike might have to teach -
though I'd come to dance and was free to go.

Letter to the Superintendent of Buildings

Dear Superintendent
I have made my inspection.
There are weaknesses
in all your best structures
such that a single voice
singing a single song
at the precisely incorrect
pitch could bring them down.

And I have seen always
one balcony above me
on the travertine staircase
a solitary male or female
I cannot tell which figure
following a torch but I
could only catch the odor of burning
pitch could bring them down.

I requested Leo and the rest
to help me track these singers
and arsonists, but Leo
has placed me in arrest
instead. He doubts my word.
I think you should speak
to him sir before we are all
pitched and brought down.

Capitalist Sonnet

This baby knows nothing at all of shame.
If he soils himself, his parent, diaper, bib,
Look! New! Excrement added!   he proclaims,
Proud of the foul excretions in his crib.

This baby is unfortunately fond of fire.
Cats' tails, pillows, relatives' linty cuffs,
Half the neighborhood he once turned pyre,
And sat in the stench of ashes proudly fireproof.

Bright marbles and live grenades are equal in his eye.
He loves bluejays and the air-raid siren's scream.
Sounds suggesting words punctuate his shrill cries,
Like the solid clots that bubble in spoiled cream.

Grace and I produced him, and where can I
Find grace and heart to let the great lubber die?

Men's Room

Easy to pity Harold Mungo
his anonymous fame
as a giver of good
blow jobs, or fat, unseen
but surely porky
Stanley Dubie,
notorious eater
of gooey shit.
O weep, for Donna Harris
gives good head,
for Fern and Vickie,
always good in bed;
for Kilroy, too,
dangling his phallic
snout over the eternal
wall that stands between
those too much in love
with love and those
with no love at all.

Skeleton Jokes

Down at the cemetery the skeletons
Are telling jokes again.
They tell a joke and they all laugh.

When skeletons laugh balloons
Of dust puff
Out around their teeth.

Skeleton jokes are like jokes
Told by close friends
Of long standing. They aren't funny -

It's the repetition. Skeletons
Don't ever change
Their jokes, not even a little.

Maybe it would be for the better,
But why should they?
Skeleton jokes are like jokes.

The Poor Capitalists Go to the Movies

The road is rutted sand
through scrubby jack pines,
sucking clay that weights
the feet, sunstruck tar
that reaches after every
step, or merciless concrete.
No matter, they must run,
zigzagging crazily as they can,
the bullets raising holes
behind them. They can
tuck and roll
into any ditch they please -
one plane barrels over
but another one is always there
to raise them up running
again on their deadened
legs, lips grabbing for
shreds of air, never
enough, never enough air.
Scraps of scenery flare
in the corners of their eyes,
extinguished before they can think
what they are, whether hands
held out from refuge
or claws extended to

trip their desperate knees.
Their view is black
from lack of breath
and in the black clouds
silver specks swim.
Such flight as this
is for soldiers, not
for these aged, shaken,
flabby limbs, these exhausted
hearts. They run
out of the theatre
of endless war, out
of this dream,
into the streets
where the strafing
starts again, and they
can run some more.

The War

(In memory of Michael Levine)

His red beard copper in the sun,
he battled patiently in the black field
against the sumac, sassafras,
Canadian thistle. For years his forehead
burned as he looked toward the oaks' cool shade
and gouged sweat from his eyes
and bent again to address his enemies.
The fine needles of the thistle
took residence in his skin
and the sumac spread in his dreams,
red veins staining the green.
But he won, finally, and the field was cleared
when he went away to war.
When he returned,
nothing had been planted,
and the sumac curled redder than his beard,
the thistles looked him in the eye,
and it was all gone to sassafras again.

Stray Fire - Vietnam, 1968

His eyes are jelly holes
The sheep his wool is fire
Toppling up the slope
Toward the wire.

No
Says the sheep's master.
He can only follow her.
The sheep goes faster.

In the wire they all rolled,
Held, holding, all defiled.
The poor girl, she foaled.
My cradle. Oh my child.

Western Haiku

The rearview mirror
rose above
a rabbit

smashed flat.
In the West, we break
to our measure.

A word in Viet-Nam
for river is song.
The rabbit is song.

In Wyoming the road
goes on, sand and sides.
The road is the end.

The road goes under
me and I go on. This is
my song, Viet-Nam.

Five Postcards Going West

La Porte, Indiana County Fair

Budu the elephant weeps
While the rubes applaud.
Budu's great forepaws fold
To a carny god.

Chicago

The glass partition rolls
On oily balls
Shut. The men's lips move.
Oh what the hell.

Denver

The seismographer records
His mother's tremors
As brother feeds the snakes
Down her pajamas.

Nampa, Idaho Roadside Vendor

The Indian keens for his squaw.
He appears to be out of luck.
Acrylic on velveteen.
Twenty-seven bucks.

Disneyland

The Tennessee farmer
Cocks his Japanese gun
And Lincoln's great head
Explodes. So long, son.

The North American Wolverine

My saliva tastes of steel
and my own blood and I
cannot throw it clear.
I thrash and it clatters and holds.
Brown flowers sink
in the snow around me and I
cannot throw it clear.
I took the easy meat.
The trap will eat me unless I
throw it clear or unless I
eat myself free.
Fear.
The black pines watch me eat.

Vegas

She sits on a bench
overhung with green
counting the concrete roses
in the casino garden
recovering from the latest
beating, waiting
for the next to start.
The Man picked her out
before she was born
looked at her from under
his lizards lids blue-jowled,
decided to kill her every day
as long as she would last.
She grows more beautiful
with every beating she withstands.
We meet in the casino garden,
try to hide, try to hope.
There is no escaping The Man,
and no amount of weeping
will make the roses
anything other than concrete.
This is where there is
for us to hold hands.

Heron

Heron weaves his neck
and his eyes stitch circles
around the marsh. Heron
has no wish ever
to be startled.
He moves in circles along
the shore, appears awkward,
never strikes until sure
of his quarry. Heron
can stand all day
in the reeds on one leg
until the riffles still
and the wind subsides
in the pines. The circle
of the sky above sways
in the circle of his yellow eye.

Five Fingers for John Berryman

I

Canyon without a wall
Rapids of silence
I was all
In that place.
I was the wall.
Faces ignited there:
Waldo and Walt,
Blake and Bones.
Call a halt.
No brake in this
Place, o Jones.
Henry would break bones
To find one in his face.

II

No more waiting
Here they are but worse.

I can't distinguish them
Anymore, not even see them.

And nurse, I call,
But there's no nurse.

They want to smother me.
Stop up my mouth, my nose.

My eyes. My ears.
They have a cork for my ass.

I've never been well.
This is the worst.

If I could get sick
I could see them again at least.

I have a thirst to see
My friends once more.

Nurse, nurse, I call.
There is no nurse.

III

They don’t make them like
They make them any more
A cheap out before they

They put crap and toadstools
Shored up with
To be leaving like

A million guitars
Manufactured in Japan

This.

IV

Three dead, rest dying up
A storm, what with the gulls
Banging noggins on slop
Of waves uniforms on breasts

Is one mighty part
Of the trouble. Mateys, you be
Zipping down your pants,
Har if you don't be.

O ay, if you don't be
One mighty wavewoman
Rises in back, you see
Her as a girl or iris,

A fern or sparrow,
Still, slap you down,
Eat your marrow, and whatever,
Boyo on deck, she's coming.

V

The hyenas have a favorite.
They spend the long afternoons
Watching him operate and they
Snigger and twitch like loons.

The loons have the same favorite.
They drift at the edge of the mist,
Watching him operate, and they
Weep and snuffle and list.

That was not Henry's favorite though,
But he came to Henry's nest
To operate on watching Henry.
And final, Bones, they kissed.

The Seventies

Nothing

Ducks on the duck pond
Doves in the locust
Rain fills the cups
Of the last crocus.

The wind on its pivot
Turns from the north,
Drives all the new grass
Flat to the earth,

Riffles the duck pond,
Freezes the rain,
Stops the green blood
Cold in the green vein.

Ducks on the duck pond
Veer toward the shore.
That which can bend
Bends to the wind's roar.

The doves remonstrate
With the brainless wind
Which has nothing to lose.
Nothing is gained.

Nada
(Translation by Eduardo Chávez)

Patos en charcos
Palomas en el algarroto
Lluvia llena las copas
Del último croco de marte.

Viento en su volteada
Hecho del norte
Fracasando las espadas de nuevo sacate,
Plano a la tierra,

Dirijiendo olas en charco de patos,
Congela la lluvia,
Para la sangre verde
Enfría la verde vena.

Patos en el charca de pato
Virados hacia la orilla.
Que puede doblar
Doblados al aire rugiriendo.

Remonstran las palomas
Con el aire sin cerebro
Que no tiene nada que perder.
Nada se gana.

The Lepers

Sent away to sandy places
they learn to eat nettles
and the spaces between the stars
teach them what it is to burn.
They know where fern grows
from speaking the desert's
diction. In the cities,
they watch through iron bars.
Pity in passing causes
them to claw at the latches
and fleer. Later they laugh,
comparing the weapons
of their affliction.

Leper Traps

They seed the clouds with middle aged
Ladies who smile cookies.
The ladies drift down onto the desert;
Their full skirts deflate; they are set.

Houris and geishas and trollops
And virtuous women are trained
To smack over their sores
As if they were not sores.

They write a drama,
Fun at the Colony ,
To see what fool lepers
Will apply to play themselves.

They plant shrunken sharp stick men,
Points smeared with opiated
Poison, in rows along the roads
That wander toward the wells.

Two lepers lurch along
Companionable and skewed,
Laughing. Their tufted heads step down
Like suns behind the sandy hill.

Sidney Greenstreet at Yale

When still a lad lithe and flanneled,
Prone to arts thought unmeet
By brawny Yale bravos,
He perpetrated this feat:

Withdrawing from its case
A violin of proven antiquity,
He hammered a home run
Far beyond propinquity

And negligently dandled
The unbroken instrument
Before the rude parvenus'
Gaping wonderment.

Henceforth puzzled respect
Followed him and he learned shame.
In later years he despised
Fungos as he despised fame.

Sidney Greenstreet at Ringside

In a lazy spray of droplets
His mouthpiece flies still
In his dreaming eyes. He pets
The canvas and looks nil
And his lips untasting kiss
The harsh salt fibers
Of his bed he dreams a breast
And his blood a cool river.

Panama white in the darkness,
The famous conniver's
Eyes in a narrowed nest
Of fat deliver
Orders which antedate
The current crisis.
"Combobulate."
His boy quivers. Rises.

His Eminence Played by Sidney Greenstreet

Not the proprietor, he nevertheless
Sits, listening or not,
To the last Harmon mute confess
The best of a bad lot.

Shadows are curled in corners,
Red neon tubing dies with a bleat.
He is not one of the mourners;
Dawn is locked out sprawled in the street.

Fastidious among the residue,
He nevertheless has an interest
In the gummy ashes that glue
The bartender's hand to the singer's breast.

Fingerprints outlast glasses.
Smoke lingers after avid lips.
An intricate construction of matchsticks
Rises between his corpulent fingertips.

Sidney Greenstreet Taken

Dusk midges do the bug dance on the slick
Smoked surface of the pond below the weir.
The light left in the trees clots thick.
Nighthawks rattle, plane and veer.

A student of grubs and pupas,
Caddis wings, black hellgrammites,
He wades the cold stream, his loops
Of line snapping like snake flight.

He loves the innocence of insects.
Equally he loves the wiles
And savagery of salmon and connects
The two on his hook at the edge of the spill.

The salmon explodes the pool.
He cannot throw the hook.
Line flees the screaming spool.
Complaints issue from shorebound ducks.

He feels the gape of darkness close
Around him as the hook sets.
Why, sir, death is the current that flows,
And I am taken. By gad, sir. Better yet.

The Servant's Grape Dream Memory

Between the two resilient skins,
Slow thumb, still finger,
She testing one resilient skin
Of a green grape.
She do not pop; she linger.

Who? to this lady loving shape
Would this grape bring her?
How? would he test this lady nape
As she the grape?
Yes: the opera singer.

When? leap from his cape and skin,
Grape, lady, singer,
Make wine, end test, to taste begin,
All outside in?
It will not stop, she linger.

The Servant's Cinema

And then the vampire, teeth in trees
She slip silk shifting snuff the lamp
An opera cape whips his long knees
Across the lawn the grass is damp.
She in the moon. She never sees.

She tenders up her tuber throat
He gurgles. I wouldn't turn my back
To anywhere. This is the terrible part,
Face flashing squawk behind the black,
Bent back. She wasn't very smart.

Where were they when there was no sun?
He's eaten the scientist's poor daughter.
Now they are angry and kill him soon,
Poor vampire. But when he caught her -
They make it be over before it's begun.

These Many Mornings

That poor man's brain
Does black beneath his eyes
These many mornings
He did try and tries
To get out of his remains.

Bitten within
He bites no matter hands
Bound to wound binding
He strains at their bands
And sins they sadden sins,

Poor man. Father,
Take some soup, she prays,
Take some fish chowder.
Your saints and people say
It is the best brain fodder.

The Servant's Dream Ballad

And dead out of nowhere marches the man
Elbow in my ribs and whiskey mutter
Excuse me, now, Miss, kiss if you can
And Jack made mention of his Mother.

A fist came down and a tooth came through
A cheek and into the running gutter
They go, saying I'll show you, you
Mother, to speak about my Mother.

I'm not your mother, Jack - but he
Was punching the man who ripped at his ear
And both of them crying with fear couldn't see
And I was beginning to disappear

And I was beginning to disappear
And How do you do? she says to Jack's mother,
I thought you dead this much of the year -
No, I don't know what's come of Jack or the other.

November Morning

Poured in a milky glass,
A luminous scarce sway
As it is carefully transported
On a leaf-scattered tray
Held loosely in stiff fingers
Through every room
Through the pale curtains
Where she was oiled and courted
Carelessly spoiled and certain
She would always hear opera singers.

Musicians
(for William Eastlake)

They will always wander around
bemused as bakers
dusted with night-flour.
They can't get it off
their hands or faces.
Don't want to.
Crazy as bakers in a town under seige,
staring mostly at nothing
the seige guns can explode.
Apartments spew mattresses and cats.
They cannot hear mattresses and cats.
They have no trade.
They are no use.
They feed people.
They will always have
nothing to lose.

The Revelers' Aeroplane Trip

[The Revelers were a male quartet who, in the late 20's and early 30's, sold more records than any musical act until the Beatles. Their material included such cheerfully racist gems as "Dusky Stevedore" and "Moonlight on the Ganges (my leee-tul hin-doo)."]

The vocal four extremely
Famous oriental pears
Emit hot harmonies,
Liver-lip careless darky cares.

After the studio, the dates
In hotels, the willing girls
Stir Gibsons, worship and wait
Pearl onion breath and pearls.

But snap suspenders, taxicabs
Must dash - the telegram
Has come, terse as Spring rain -
So long, too short, you lovely gams.

Salvation Army commands
You appear amid motheaten furs,
Stained mattresses and used umbrellas.
Yassuh. So solly, fellahs. Yassuh.

Ornithology

People remember Charlie Parker
Rode into Minton's on a horse
Dressed in overhauls
Lip drooping a piece of straw.

People remember Charlie Parker
Hocking his alto for a fix
Living just anywhere
Raving out of control down a rainy street.

People remember Charlie Parker
Worked with the higher extensions
Of the chords, worked with strange
Intervals, unheard-of overtones.

People remember Charlie Parker
He was the one invented Bop,
A movement toward wide lapels,
Pegged trousers and peculiar talk.

People can't remember a bird
In flight they've never seen.
Pocketa ta pocketa ta pocketa pock.
Klactoveedsedstene.

Dexter

Little smiling geeks,
Large tattooed arthropods,
Hair up their white collarbones
Bouncing racist dangles,

Old women suddenly sisters
Beside you on the bus,
All of them talking
Their shit at once,

And what beautiful combination
Can become their melody
Tonight?

Something Elegant

A white page
A black brush
A page at Windsor Castle
A black brush-off
A worker
A worker reading

Elegance seems to reside
at our fingertips

Charlie Parker's long,
flat fingers
Muhammed Ali's fists
writing poems

Picasso's brush
Hepburn's blush
Dickinson's pages
Dostoievski's rages

Elegance
Seems to reside
at our fingertips

Little Moments in Intellectual History:
Emerson

Emerson strides through brick red Boston,
Brick yellow Boston, Boston grey
And brown with Autumn,
White hair spuming from his crown,
Overcape splaying its flaps,
Talking to much unpresent company.
Emerson is of the angry mad
When he gets off on one of his walks
Like this.
                    Boomstraddle, ipswitchays!
See, I make words for you.
They tell you what to do,
And what you are. They connote
How unpleasant your presence
With me is to me.
The truth passes through me
And you try to fit it with locks
In a fit of fear.
Fff-Fff-ff-fuh -
If the red slayer thinks he slays!
Let him who has ears to hear,
Hear.

Blue Light

Blue light through the window falls
On the silver kitchen fixtures.
He pours himself one last drink,
Carefully closes down the faucet.

His past leers at him from the walls.
There's no way out of his own stink,
Nothing for his tongue but his own dentures.

One memory only: once, when she spread
Her legs, the little Indian girl -
He thinks, getting his mouth around the barrel -
The little Indian girl who smiled as she lost it.

Magritte's Flaming Tuba

Neruda has unexpectedly dropped
Into my bathtub. Hello, Neruda,
It is a great pleasure to meet you.
Magritte's flaming tuba

And now this, Neruda dapper
In spite of the sodden condition
Of his immaculate business suit,
Speaking his precise, gentle sedition.

We converse of this tub, which
Neruda entered without a splash,
No Roman monstrosity but just
A tub. A faucet. Drain. Ceramic soapdish.

Dawn wakes like a frozen fly
In the dust on the sash. Improbable
As peace, we sit in our senses, Neruda
And I, happy as Romans in rubble,

While the sky washes its elbows
And the old whore blinks herself chaste.
We bow low to this room where all
Is perfectly human as Neruda's face.

Magritte's Bogus Sausages

His knees protrude like roots
From a stream from the surface of his bath.
He lies submerged in his suit.
His fingers easily as willow shoots

Meet in a dome before his sight.
This is uncommonly daft,
Even for you, remarks his bride,
Disparagement born of delight.

Magritte says nothing. His focus
Both far and near reveals
A sausage linked at the locus
Of two fingertips, a manifest bogus

Sausage. Curious, Magritte
Produces two more. He feels
There is nothing in such a feat.
One must, when all is said, eat.

Les Professeurs Dangereuses

On the green enamel tabletops
Individual pearls of rain quiver
As black umbrellas float by
In the invisible river.

Magritte sits at a table in the rain,
Allowing nothing to pass
Unnoticed. His eyes absorb more light
Than the black pool of his demi-tasse.

Among the miraculous lumps
Borne by umbrellas, several professors
Stand stranded like barkless logs.
Ach, they savor, Was ist besser?

Each holds his head up with a strap
Grown from ear to ear.
Occasionally they exchange heads.
Always they are exceedingly sincere.

The silver rain avoids them
As they debate whether Magritte
And such unfortunates should be
Killed with kindness. Pourquoi non? Dit.

Botticelli's Aphrodite

None of the rest is worthy, not
The maiden aunt's sofa flowers,
Not the cardboard waves
Or the trumpetless trumpeter

Who floats buoyant as anchors,
His dead doxy stiff in his ideas
Of arms, expectorating messages
Concerning a comfortless breeze.

Her flesh not flesh, her hair
Harsh as a cheap doll's wig,
She will never move
Anyone. Her toes are too big.

All of the rest is nothing
More than curlicues to frame
Her eyes which break your eyes
For what you practice in her name.

The Invention

Oh brother give me five, Gabriel
Grins through his diamond tooth.
Michael splays his thighs
And laughs too hard to make a sound.
Farina rubs his belly
And smiles his wise old evil smile, and
Fetchit's face spreads like the dawn,
Slowly. God doesn't say a word,
Just all the time signifies.

Poor Adam and poor Eve
Cling to each other,
Blessed and deaf
To all but each other's cries.
It is impossible for it to last.
Poor Adam and poor Eve.

But, too, God is God
Because later
He gives them to laugh.

Pedagogical Stukas

This is three ravens demonstrating geometry,
Physics, three-point and aerial perspective.
Suddenly, immediately and convincingly, the ravens
Appear and approach and attain their objective.

Light fingers bare rocks on the flowered shoulder.
Then the three ravens. No more connection
Than between good weather and colder.
Colder takes office. No election.

Hands in your armpits, say the ravens.
This is a test you did not pass.
Here are the answers: Warm, no. Havens,
No. Pedagogical stukas, yes.

Tennis in Tornado Time

You and your brown legs
at tennis in the dusk.
Gales plaster the bridal pleats
to your vaulting vault.
Twisters finger trees
on all horizons,
trailer courts explode babies and crockpots,
shoats rocket out of sight
like dirigible golf balls.
None of it deters you.
Giggle and pat and hip it
to the forecourt,
keeping no score,
making no points,
marking no faults.

Hitler for Dinner

I invite Hitler for dinner.
I want more strange eyes
White and mad as ermine
Shimmering obtuse as flies

Bothering my beloved faces.
I contemplate Hitler's forelock
And ridiculous mustache
Dropping hairs in the soup crock.

To accompany the vinaigrette
He provides a drum of boots
At the door and distant screams
To savor the asparagus shoots.

Now he is at the bookcase with a poker.
Froth and scraps of first
Editions well from his lips
Swollen fat as wurst.

This is the first of many
Difficult little dinner parties.
I doubt my ability to remain
Composed, let alone hearty.

If he is my friend, how
Can my friends quail and shudder?
If he is my enemy,
Who are these others?

Hitlerian Scrabble

Hitler is hell on company.
They keep leaving early, because and in spite
Of his rheumy-eyed, canine
Attempts at gemutlichkeit.

We of course try to draw him in
In order to draw him out. We babble
Tense as the bachelor uncle left with the baby.
Someone suggests a game of Scrabble.

Our strained enthusiasm has a short
Half-life, but our new friend
Immediately loves this pastime
Which he refuses to comprehend.

Rolling his eyes he drops his jaw
To bellow triumph as he slaps
Our wooden trays of letters
Into our undefended laps

And plays his PZX and proudly
Counts points on his stubby fingers.
So much for edifying games.
The guests go for the coat hangers.

All but one. Undeniably present
As a sulphurous eggfart, Hitler remains,
Cheerful as a knee-humping dog,
Peasant sly, victoriously inane.

Hitler Curled in His Alcove

He delights in surreptitious phone calls.
We are likely to discover at any hour
Hitler curled in his alcove, eyes
Vague as teenagers' until he glowers
Up and gestures us away, his hand
Peremptory as a homecoming queen's.
Ostentatiously not speaking to the black
Receiver nestled in the crotch between
His cocked head and pointed shoulder,
He waits pointedly. We go away.
This is a good excuse for amused
Contempt and fond parental dismay.
That rascal. What can these long whispers
And muttered giggles portend?
We are not sure that all this talk
Is healthy, but at least he has friends.
We close the bedroom door. We could
Easily lift the receiver from the bedside
Telephone. We turn out the light.
Lie breathing in the dark terrified.

Guestroom for Hitler

He sits in his room for days,
Hands clasped in the small lap
Made by his crossed stub legs,
Cold and alone as a childhood map
Of the South Pole. The philodendron
Rimes and pales. Grandmother's afghan
Fades. Papa's humidor bleeds
Copper and grows grey as a steel ashcan.

He will rise from this funk strutting,
Spitcurl black as penguins against snow,
Filled with the poor room he has left etched
So deep that only the shadows show.

Winter 1944

The sky of French winter
Settles on tile roofs.
Black oaks open and splinter
And heave, silently cuffed

By shrapnel on a far hill.
Villagers scurry under their plumes
From door to door and lesser generals
Sit worrying in commandeered rooms.

Colonels pass brandy to majors.
There is much talk of strategy.
Fear lights cigarettes and labored
Tactics blurt from startled proteges.

In the cellar of the butcher
Ike juggles three wooden balls.
Smooth as black market butter,
One rises as another falls.

In Huertgen Forest death bellows
And thrashes, blood flows in brown trenches
In the snow. Ike juggles in the cellar.
Tout. Rien. Ike often thinks in French

Of what must be done. Practice.
Cold as the limestone of these buried walls.
One must escape all tactics.
Two hands. At least three balls.

Ticker Tape

Another celebration.
All the workers in God's office building
Chucking confetti
Into the convection above the trees.

Although it is less than morning,
And said trees are barely
Umber diagrams
Of one thousand or more previous afflictions.

However no account is
No account, the workers remain
Away from their desks
All day feigning pleasure to please

God who has ordered up
This celebration for obscure purposes.
Later on
The trees get drunk drinking God's praise.

Shirley Temple Kaleidoscope

Millions of identical amber bottles
Borne like chunky potentates or friars
Toddle along in the steel river
Each neck gripped by steel pliers.

Or no. A galaxy is dynamited
And all the gaseous sunrise
Flowers, cobalt, ultramarine,
Orange petals settle together like flies.

Or several dead babies float
Down between the waterlogged pilings,
Like sinister balloons in the greenish
Slop, smiling smiling smiling.

Shirley stamps NO to that
And gives a good shake to the tube.
She is a perfectly curly organization
And in addition is all good.

Look again. Before a stucco
Governmental office like a stack
Of blinding salt, a petulant
Africanissimo stares back.

He shakes his tube, and Shirley
Is a suddenly particularly bright
Shard of what she thought
She observed as you as I who this write.

Shirley's Rat

The rat breaks sprockets in time,
Was there is here is there.
He carries razors in his cheeks' pockets,
Plague lice in his gritty hair.

Intent as adolescent genius,
He solves cellars and sewers.
All that is scorned and wasted
And spent is the rat's sinecure.

Shirley shudders and shakes her glass
To dispel this grizzled, burly,
Busy image, but that perfect devil
The rat merely breaks wind securely.

So Shirley smashes her tube,
Primly deposits it in the trash,
Never to see the rat grown great
Gorging on broken glass.

Should Hope Kiss a Toad?

Should Hope kiss a toad
is continuously a puzzle,
as pop eyes abound
and sewn gapes of muzzle.
Scrawny limbs may grow lithe
or may remain scrawny.
Distended pots may never
tighten smooth and bonny.

Hope scratches her various
tight curls and looks serious.

What if no dance emerges
from these throttled leaps?
What if for song is only
more basso-contralto rrreeps?
The dumb, malevolent stare
of fear may never melt,
nor electric soft skin
replace obnoxiously nubbed pelt.

Hope nips her perfect thumbnail
in her perfect smile.

Her eyes may recede and blink
forever, and her limbs
may stay fat, and she may always
shriek saccherine hymns.
How can she fail disaster
with her unpondering lope?
She will provide few insects.
Should a toad kiss Hope?

Frog Baron Problems

Feckless couriers, inexplic,
Part of every day's complex
Transacts. Neck swoll hard as jade,
Frog Baron pouts - not perplexed,

No, no, no, no. Frog Baron is frogselfmade.
He does not ponder, he elects
The next best, next worst trick.
"Got to expect some losses," he reflects.

But tender moments? Yes, of course -
All the shopworn, holy staples:
Tadpoles swarming welcome home,
Buffa the Nun-Frog, Mom in her wimple.

Occasionally a pop eye blows,
Geysering transmogrified flies,
Souping the spectators' lapels.
The seller sells; the buyer buys.

Feckless couriers, aborted deals,
Rates rising.... Tendons flex,
Rigid as jade, hard as green steel.
Moving flies is hard; it is complex.

Pride, that each day the marsh is fed -
This is Frog Baron's only prize,
The only duty to which he bends.
Not easy. It is not easy, moving flies.

Ecclesiastes

He hides the bass drum in the forest.
He soaks the tent with crazy juice.
He hires and corrupts a chorus
Of testifying virgins and bogus Sioux.

The tent glows like a floating stove,
Swells like an orange heart.
The vox humanum groans,
And then the staggering whoops start.

He observes when their collars splay
In frenzy, their eyes scum over
Adoringly and their lips spray,
Attentive as a young lover.

He drinks yokel sweat.
He hears sorrow and is clement.
He covers the entire bet.
He does not live in the tent.

Yokels

They do not live in the tent.
They live in villages in pine woods.
They live feeling the earth slant,
And still plow and still sell goods.

Some of them torture dogs
In the spent dust of alleyways;
Eviscerate squirming polliwogs;
Use shotguns on blue jays.

Some of their hands are carved
Rigid as oak to the fit of tools.
Some shoulders bear a curve
Tight as the collars on the mules.

They employ a despised teacher
To mark wrists with a rule.
They distrust their own natures.
They give no credence to fools.

Dun rabbits crouch in tufts
In the winter fields; killdeer
Cry and nest in the clods, bereft
Of their buff shelter.

This must do and will not.
Debts incurred in innocence
Cannot be covered in the hot
Night beneath the uninhabitable tent.

En La Casa Fuentes

The green of the wig of the man
In the booth at the front is bile.
The teeth of the girl of the green-wigged man
Appear to have tasted of the file.
Four drunken persons whoop
In the corner near the kitchen doors,
Accusing each other of tedious achievements.
Their tongues are on all fours.
The murals have begun to move.
The waitresses' feet sink in the planks.
The guitarist's strings snap in his face.
Whole sacks of onions are rotted rank.
Fuentes it no longer amuses.
Whether a bubble, burst on the sun,
Or certain planets conjoined,
Or the devil or the demon rum
Or all combined have instigated chaos
In his house, Fuentes cares not.
He contemplates the unrhythmic din
Silently, gives a brief nod,
And rises. Fuentes walks.
Between the tables, to the kitchen,
Grave and erect as Sunday
He proceeds without expression.
The tongues of the drunkards stagger
To their feet. The floor releases

The waitresses. The murals stop.
In the kitchen Fuentes teases
The cook, then returns to his place.
About the girl with the pointed dientes
Nothing need be done. Anyone
May be served at La Casa Fuentes.

Test Pilot
(for Matt McGrath)

He puts up with the brass,
with waddling bearlike in his clumsy wrappings,
with grey men who talk,
with talk, talk, talk, with talk.

Waddling bear-light in his suit
out on the runway slab,
he can grin inside his bubble.
Waiting to smile is part of the price.

The plane coils up quivering like a cat
on its hot invisible haunches
and springs at the ghost of the moon
in the pale grey desert sky.

Down in the flat, squat, sand-splattered
concrete blockhouse,
finance and politics salivate
in the agony of their greed.

A black whip cracks.
Trees quail and writhe toward the whirling ground.
He has entered the silence that sings
beyond the barrier of sound.

The Great Nagurski's Blocking Guard

(for Alec, Big Earl, and Little Earl)

Alec Bobedash, the great Nagurski's
blocking guard, stands at the stern
bent to raise the outboard motor
over the sandy bottom ferns.
The channel widens, bottom falls
away. In northern morning haze
the slow prow slides rising
onto Shishebogama, lake of many bays.
Then the long run over the deep
center, the outboard motor cut,
the shore pines faint through the mist,
Bobedash testing the anchor knot.
Unwatching he watches the shore
for the crooked finger of the broken dock,
pointing, as he then points,
toward the great blue heron on the rock.
The party of fishermen stirs in the cold.
Bobedash, without regret or wish
or thought of Nagurski, grunts
at the endless mystery of the fish.
They think I guide they think
I know they think I think.
The rope plays in his old hand.
He watches the anchor drink.

The Talking Toaster Owner Talks
(After a Jack Ziegler cartoon, New Yorker, 1/5/76. You could look it up.)

Of course they make a good deal of fun
Of me. I understand that.
If you have never heard a toaster talk,
Tell you things, things
Worth listening to, things
In your own language,
How could you be brave enough
Not to laugh?

Glow is comforting in morning black.
Warm your front and warm your back.
Toast is born as the bread dies.
All waiting is worthy to the wise.

No, and if a person has never heard
The water talking in the pipes,
How will that person know
How like the water's talk is
To the language he spoke once
In a dream he woke to hear?
In that dream he uttered the perfect poem,
Beautiful to raise the hair
All over the body,
Which to his wakened ear was gibberish.

Of course, it was water talk.

I only wish them more fun in their fun.
That is why I appear in these cartoons -
Magnanimity. I am magnanimous.
It shows I think
Confidence
The confidence yes I feel
Quite confident.

Running and standing still.
Am I up or down the hill?
I am the liquid mutter of the blaze,
The same poem so many different ways.

In the Grey Evening Which May Rain
(for Ikuo Ihara)

Around the earth's blue rind,
I look down at the top
of your head, a black comma
in the court of pruned trees.
You stroll in the grey evening
which may rain. Chrysanthemums
glow salmon and soft
as earlobes. Invisible
parasites and hidden roots
are pulverizing the courtyard,
the flat stones powdered
with themselves. A kitten
examines a dead twig.
You watch alone, smiling
only inside your face. Look over
the shrugging shoulder of the world.
I am down here, sitting
in the grey evening which may rain.

En La Noche Gris Que Podrá Llover
(Translation by Eduardo Chávez)

Sobre un aura de azul cubriendo este mundo,
Veo tu cabello bajo de mí
Como una marca de puntuación
En el cortejo de árboles podados.
Andas en la noche gris
Que podrá llover. Crisántemas
Dan luz de salmón y suaves como
Lobulos. Invisibles los parásitos
Y raíces escondidas machacan el
Sequito, piedras planas polvorizadas
Con ellas mismas. Un gatito
Explora una varilla seca.
Ves, sin compañía, sonriendo
Solamente dentro de tu cara. Trata
Con indiferencia el levantado hombro
Del mundo. Estoy aquí, sentado
En la noche gris que podrá llover.

The Buddha's Funeral

Here is the Buddha's funeral.
The elephants weep and wobble,
Peacocks droop broken umbrellas,
Mice pound their fists on the cobbles.

Here the monks in saffron cassocks
Gnash teeth and squinch their eyes,
Competing in woe, as the Buddha
Goes up in the smoke of his pyre.

These are the troops, slashing
And falling beneath sharp hooves
In one of the famous battles
For possession of the Buddha's tooth.

These are the infamous cats,
Mousing, curling, sleeping
Through the Buddha's funeral,
Yawning amid general weeping.

This is the Buddha, watching
These slides most fit and fat,
Feet sunk in his hassock,
Cradling numerous cats.

Nothing

The air is soaked with dusk
And the fallen apple petals
Lie blue on the grass.
The spiked heads of nettles

Stand in the sounding angelus.
I stand with the hose.
The water wells and bubbles
In the manure beneath the rose.

Blobs grave as mercury
Of water tremble
On rose leaves. These
Pools reflect the temple.

This is no different from the world
I saw before I saw the world.
The robin's night call leaves
Nothing to be inferred.

Nada
(Translation by Eduardo Chávez)

Empapado el aire con el anochecer
Y los pétales de manzana
Se acuestan azules en el pasto con
Las espigadas cabezas de ortiga,

Para en el ángelus sonante.
Me paro con la manguera.
El agua charca y brotea
En el abono bajo la rosa.

Burbujadas tan graves como mercurio
De agua tiemblan
Sobre hojas de rosas. Estos son las
Lagunas que reflejan el templo.

Esto no es diferente que el mundo
Que vi antes que vi el mundo.
En la noche, la llamada del petirrojo no deja
Nada de ser inferido.

The Eighties

Improved Octopus

I hereby invent
an improved octopus.
He reaches out
through his selfmade murk
filled with swirls of meat,
tiny shimmering tidbits
which are not him,
little glimmers of sun
in the sepulchral gloom
of octopus life,
he reaches out
and eats every goddam
speck of light or life
he can consume.
All right.
So he's not improved.

The Latest Long Goodbye

In Altman's version of The Long Goodbye,
Elliott Gould as Philip Marlowe
slouches the streets that look like B-lot sets,
registers it all - the swingers' tits hanging out,
the speedfreaks become respectable
hooking the whole culture, the cops
nakedly kicking ass for the temporarily powerful,

all of it - with values inside him
smelted in the 1940s,
unbroken though not undented
by forty more years of seeing it all,

all the time mumbling to himself,
"It's all right with me. It's all right with me.
It's all right with me." But of course
it is not all right. He can't numb himself
sufficiently to yield to what we've become.
He can't kill or evade his anger.
So he keeps almost getting himself killed,
a samurai in the Toyota factory.

It's not all right until Marlowe makes it all right
with his gun. Hooray for Hollywood.

Colorful
(for Bob Blaze)

Until Long-Gone Miles,
replete with too-good weed,
came crashing down face forward
from the stage,

everything was going well enough
for the tourists having colorful
drinks in a colorful place, the bus
idling at the curb,

ready to take them back
to their hotel in predictableland.
Then here came Miles, cheap tabletops
cracking, collapsing,

drinks all over and broken glass,
Miles bleeding on them,
clawing at their taffeta
as he attempted to cope.

Real blood, leaving brown stains
on the seersuckers.
As if Lincoln from his marble chair
looked suddenly down

and said, “Pissants!
Who are these pissants, there,
frightened little things
crawling all over my republic?”

Disentangled from Long-Gone’s
reality, they made it for the Grey Line.
Miles was out of a gig again,
needless to say.

Boudu Saved From Drowning

Boudu, the old tramp at the table,
saved from drowning by his bourgeois host,
spills blood-brown wine on the tablecloth
and sees his savior's wife spill salt
upon it, to draw it from the linen.
She is very quick with the salt,
her mouth a prune of concentration.

The dinner declines, nerves fray,
the host's son knocks over the salt cellar,
and Boudu, logic impeccable,
purses his lips and drowns the spilled salt
with wine. He senses a mistake.
Before he tried to drown himself,
even his dog had given up on him.
This day will not end.

Gaper's Block

In the median ahead
a big car has rolled,
spewing the contents of another
desperate moving day
out over the burned grass.

Naturally everyone throttles down
to gape at this
banal tragedy.
They forget all else.
One of them tries to kill me

in his idiot haste to decelerate
and park and gape,
offering nothing, gape,
learning nothing,
gape. Schwaaaa.

This is one of many phenomena
that puzzle me as I pass
among my fellow citizens.
If a string quartet
of angels had been playing back there,

all those rubbernecks
would have stiffened and sped up
to escape
any brush
with unexpected beauty.

The Great Lakes Terminal Warehouse

They say that when you see any random set of words
to be a poem, you are teetering on the ledge
of psychosis, or whatever the label is this year
for the canvas sport coat and the razor
that starts shaving once it's up your nose.
So when I see the Great Lakes Terminal Warehouse
through the window in the dawn, I let my head
jolt on into the Toledo Station. Toledo. Toledo.
I say the name to myself, trying to overtrack
the other and the poem it wants to make.

The same failed, frightened Leading Man
who sold me gin throughout the night
this morning sells me cheese danish
wrapped in molybdenum and coffee distilled
from pond scum and dead Honduran three-year-olds.
We compare a couple of notes, he looking
over his shoulder. Somehow, the Mayor of Philadelphia
who has bombed his own city comes up,
and we agree that back when we were boys,
when the buffalo and the Nazis roamed,
if someone bombed your city, if was safe to assume
he must be the enemy.

Boarding at this place, a dad, a mom,
a boy, come to see off mom's mom,
all of them sprouts from the same packet of seeds,
thin, strong, drawn slightly forward over their centers,
like bows long strung.
They part with few words, and grandma
sits down, secure within the invisible cocoon
of their powerfully unstated love.
Just some once-ordinary Americans,
who haven't yet caught up with the national progress
toward utter self-loathing.

I consider the residue lining my empty cup
as we jolt into our departing glide.
Someone announces through the Public Address System,
"We have a sick child on board
who requires Valium. If you have any Valium,
would you please come to the lounge car."
I don't have any Valium, and I'm already there.
There is no sign of a sick child. There is only me,
and Hollywood, and other sick adults.
The cornfields mandala by the window.
The Great Lakes Terminal Warehouse
was just a building in Toledo,
Toledo, the city we have left behind.

Skunk

Whoever they were,
they didn't swerve to miss you,
old girl,
as you crossed the asphalt
waving your white flag.

Their mighty, screaming tank
crushed you, drove your fine hair
right into the cold tar.
You're just a pink and white pile
still steaming on the morning street.

Already the magpies hop
on the white meridian
bright-eying your leavings,
impatient
for rush hour's end.

That rue perfume you depended on
to repel false friends
lingers in my car as I drive on.
It did you no more good than
your friendly banner in the end.

Parents' Song

Go out and play.
Stay inside the fence.
If anybody at all offers you
anything at all, tense yourself,
run, don't take it, call us instead.

Go out and play.
Slip through the fence.
If we come calling you,
run down the street, calling
the savage dogs,
the blood-drained winos,
the very cars, themselves,
to your defense.

The White Bear

An early memory she had, her mother
holding her body up
to her father's large face.

That man, such an odd presence
that smelled so various, left
one day, as she looked back,

without his peeling suitcase, and that
was when the new dads started.
Herb, the quiet victim Mom and I

got to torment together. Jack,
the one who came and went so fast
I can't remember his face.

Thurlow.
The next one she married.
One night in my room I met Thurlow.

The next morning at breakfast,
all three together
playing let's pretend.

I remember my seventh birthday,
the big white bear that was mine,
suddenly.

Onofre

Once
I dove screaming happily
into the great ocean
boiling beneath.

The great ocean accepted me
and then broke
my back for me
as a lesson.

My mother cuts the fish
that arrive, and I
watch the sky
from the beach at night.

Dying Turtle

Through my grainy slits,
I see my brothers still cavorting,
Turning their tedious cartwheels,
Crying silently, "Take me in."
They wish to be liked.

The management paints us -
Conventional scenes,
Supposedly resonant of turtleness:
Palm trees, orange sun globs,
Various unlikely fishes.

We are dying, but attractive,
We hope. Can't breathe
Through the paint. The management
Hopes we will attract
Quicker than we die.

We hope we will attract
One who will wash us,
So we turn tedious cartwheels
When the noses smear
Against the insurmountable glass.

Situation Comedy

First the characters must be established,
which in practice means
repeating a few turns of speech,
a few obvious mannerisms:

a butter voice and a lecherous eye,
a tuck of the chin and a nervous cough,
a booming delivery from a hollowed gut,
a quick intelligence above those tits.

Then, when the stereotypes are set,
each one can be developed.
Seasons can be spent in this,
if the stereotypes meet approval.

The honey-tongued libertine
lays it on the line for liberation,
the unalienable right of those tits
to get a PhD in Swinburne;

The nervous cough presages a speech
of such authority on behalf
of something good that all the other
caricatures go dumb in freeze-frame;

The popinjay assumes a sudden
dignity, living up to his pretensions;
the wastrel surprises everyone
by a display of fine moral discrimination.

These changes can go on for years,
yes, but there's a drag on them.
The stereotypes, the chords of the song
on which they improvise, don't change;

nobody wants them to change.
But the choruses must keep going,
until only the improbable riffs remain.
Improbability only goes so far,

they start saying no show runs forever,
and sometime during some summer,
a decision is made at the higher level,
and everyone is next seen

emptying desk drawers into whisky
cartons, sweeping rows of costumes
off the rods, drinking heavily, kissing
as passionately as there is, and that's it.

How to Board Your Flight at O'Hare International

After you've checked your baggage,
descend to the moving sidewalk.
It will carry you through the tunnel,
made airy and bearable by pastel
neon tubes in waving forms above,
and the lights will flow with you.

As you approach the terminal,
you will hear a voice endlessly
repeat: "The moving sidewalk
is coming to an end; please look down...
The moving sidewalk
is coming to an end;
please look down..."
The neon tubes above are winking their last.

You look up. Above the escalator,
a mirrored wall looks back. The legs
of the passengers ahead of you
pass up behind the bottom of the mirror,
toward more light, and disappear.
Presumably,
they are going to fly.

Los Alamos

Fat Man's replica,
the big death's first egg,
is polished and buffed
like a Jemez pot, and white.
Ceiling white, though,
not the white of a Jemez pot, not
the white made from a special place
in the surrounding earth.

Little Boy is well named,
inflated younger brother,
olive as only the Army
could interpret olive,
the olive in Death's martini,
a bullet with a square tail,
the arrow and the mace in one.
They lie quietly side by side
in Los Alamos, where such intense
activity produced their originals,
in the Science Museum.

Another display demonstrates
the reduction in size of the computers
used to produce the bombs
with ever greater yields.
The smaller the electronic brain,

the greater the capacity for destruction.
The big, early computers
could only destroy part of a city.

The motel has a year-round pool.
You get to it through the Spring blizzard
across the parking lot, after you've walked
halls air-conditioned outside every room.
Your key fits your motel-room door,
but does not unlock it. For your convenience,
there is one ice machine by the front door
in the lobby, where, since the machine is broken,
it will be convenient for the sadsack
deskclerk to explain that it is broken
and no ice is available.
They have ice up the street.
Every street sign is hidden
behind a pole, often one holding
another street sign.
The motel has a deli.
Slim Jims and Mars Bars.

The museum has two terra cotta statues,
General Groves and Oppenheimer, white
as textured ghosts, anatomically accurate,
and photographs of many tests, science
in action. Aniweetok. Mark I. A film
about Trinity. It's an art film, santeros
interspersed with holocaust victims

and, of course, the heroic scientists
who said, “Yes, I will do this,
because if I don’t, someone else will.”
The film is called
The City That Never Was.

The Abridgment of Hope
(in the 6th Year of Reagan)

All over the country, children are killing themselves.
In Jefferson County, Colorado, seven in four months have gone.
Go ahead: make a poem out of that - you're a poet.

Start with the seven astronauts,
whose abrupt expirations triggered an orgy
of amazed outrage, exhorbitant grief, stunned disbelief,
and other symptoms of our stubborn denial
that we all got to go. Helicopters
battered the waves, searching the sea
for the detritus of those deaths.
Implications of great import were pointed out
by those paid to point out.
Mourning was universal,
so it was said.

But over Jefferson County,
no helicopters. No commentators. No President.
No preachers. No search for causes. Nothing.
No taxes spent that these seven children
Might Not Have Died in Vain.
Just seven dead children, good
for a wrap-up on page ten, below the fold.

If they had but had the wit to band together
and blow themselves to Kingdom Come in a bunch,
they might have made page one. Had they taken off

a few dozen innocent bystanders, they would
have achieved status as terrorists.
Then even the President would have paid his brief attention.

But no, no swift incendiary glory,
no companionship in death for them.
One by one, the children found life untenable
and went away, one by one.
They found life in America, a land
tall, strong, and proud, so it is said,
not worthy of their continued attendance.
Guns being readily available,
they got their explosions, one by one.

Children three years old are killing themselves,
so it is said. They find their lives untenable.
They embrace the abridgment of hope.
Make a poem out of that. Go ahead.
Imagine yourself into a three-year-old
so worldly wise, so well informed, he knows
what suicide is, and how to commit it,
and chooses it. Who fully comprehends despair.
Go ahead.

The dead toddler is a fact.
My country's drugged preoccupation
with what, it is told, is vitally important,
the inexhaustible kaleidoscope of crises,
comedies, titillating scandals, games of greed,
perpetual touchdowns - that preoccupation
is a fact. The children die unnoticed.

How many of them, dead by our own guns,
will be required? When will we unplug ourselves,
ask what these children see, that they find life untenable?
Ask where they learn so much about despair, about resignation,
about cowardice, about cheap drama? Ask how it is that they are so alone
they embrace death for company, abridging our only hope.

Children tell lies.
Children never lie.

Conversation About Animals

Yes, we do like cats.
Yes, we like cats and dogs.
I like cats better than dogs, myself.

Yes, we like birds, too.
No, it wouldn't be a good idea
to touch birds.

Because birds don't like to be touched by us.
So if you find a bird that lets you touch it,
chances are it's sick, got some bad bugs.

I don't know. They just don't.
Maybe they remember
what usually happens when we touch them.

An Increasingly Unusual Occurrence

My sister took in a cat once from the fields,
a big Siamese male long gone feral,
who'd decided to center his activities
somewhere the outcomes were predictable.

He was not predictable, a wild cat
who'd spent his years killing little animals,
swaddled in abandonment, a diamond
who'd never heard word one about rings,

And when my sister's other cats saw him,
they put their paws to their eyes,
and he walked among them,
stalking the counter to the food bowl

like a Roman through the Britons
or an American through almost anywhere once,
and the carefully created systems
the cats had developed fell.

Dying Shark

Something is broken inside
I can't pivot left
I can't smell the blood
I can't hear in the dark

I can't hear the flutters
Of the distressed
In the dark

The meat drifts down
From pale heaven
I can't properly open my mouth
It sinks out of sight
And I can't get down after it

Toothless dolphins
I'm broken
This is ridiculous
They bump me again and again
toothlessly
What is wrong?
They should stop bothering me
Then I could decide
What is wrong
I don't understand

Leaving the Kid

The bluest bar in the world,
called “City Lights,”
has a stained, flophouse wahine,

half shimmying, half just
collapsing,
painted on its crumbling adobe flank.

“City Lights”
could be called “The Gateway
to Truth or Consequences, New Mexico,”

and the road in is the same
as the road out.
Many layers of grey today

socked down over every horizon,
the nearest hills
hemming you as you drive

through winter in the desert.

The Silence

Grief is such a silence
and the scimitar moon
has fallen already
behind the mountain.

Once over a beaver pond
outside Fairplay, I saw
a full moon set,
and as it disappeared,

a flash of silver outlined
the whole black rim
in both directions.
I swear I saw that.

Tonight it's only black,
and the silence is greater
for some unseen joker's
footsteps on the wet sidewalk.

To Sons In Case

In case, I send you these compromising photographs
of me en flagrante. Not just peccadilloes, you notice,
but me drunk, cannily vicious as a wolverine, me
corrupting friendships with casual aplomb for selfish
purposes.

In case these photographs are too faded and foxed,
here's me watching the strikers' heads slump under the
clubs
of the cops I hired. In this one, I clasp the helpless brown
ankles
while one of my buddies holds down her wrists. And
here I am putting babies in a box.

I don't want you to hate me. I'm no monster. Or,
if I am, you won't find many who aren't. Not here,
not there. Not there, either. No, I send these
remembrances
to balance your affections, so that you will know who I am,
in case I ever try to send you to liquidate the monsters.

Valentine Veggies
(for Yevgeny Yevtushenko)

The free Wednesday newspaper waits in my mailbox,
a wrapper for advertisements by the shrill ream,
topped by a sheaf of messages from New York
addressed to Occupant, my pet name.

"Valentine Veggies Keep the Heart Beating,"
the newspaper boldly asserts. A perfect story for today,
pushing slow products under the banner of health,
devoid of any taint of controversy.

The news stinks, not of of newsprint but of The Pitch,
the clamorous, incessant pitch for More,
the single story that we can have it all,
all of it cheaper, better, newer, older, all at The Big Store.

How can I give you a valentine,
in these days of the justly foundering empire,
which does not stink of The Pitch,
when every word's a whore stood out for hire?

The pen I'd write with would promote a music store, a
garage,
a sixty-buck-a-night flop house, a politician,
a florist, an endangered species, a college,
    a marriage counselor, a crazy god, a mortician,

The paper I'd write on half-visibly reveal
its maker's repellent acronym, the stamp I'd lick
carry a false, nostalgic portrait
of some simpering Norman Rockwell hick.

We live as a people conquered, our loves
corrupted by the victors' well-paid flacks.
Their blatant secret police spy in our homes,
leaving the spittle of manipulation like snail tracks

On the sill of every bedroom, every nursery,
cajoling us unceasingly to embrace greed,
to forget truth, ignore our hearts and brains,
supplicate The Big Store to fill prefabricated needs

Until there is nothing to breathe but the pitch,
and virtue's only a package for some salesman's vice,
all promises are empty, and we learn,
in self-defense, every slick, dishonorable device -

And naturally suspect our dearest must
(because who does not?) know all the tricks too.
Who can say or hear, without the inner twist
of doubt, or self-doubt, the terrible words, “I love you?”

Those Rats

When rats drop off a sinking ship
They don't think, "This ship is sinking!"
That thought would require an Einstein
Of what passes for rat thinking.

By then, they're all around the bend,
Dumbstruck or homicidal;
They'd follow each other over a cliff,
Like those Gadarene swine in the Bible.

When the flood first showed its foaming tongue,
Those rats thought, "Well, okay!
This little flood is bound to wash
Some little fancy trash our way."

But as the flood got serious
And approached the waterline,
And available space got precious,
And the air got a little fine,

One rat after another rat,
As the lightbulbs shorted blue,
Started to veer and savage,
Doing like the big rats do,

Tearing morsels from the lips of rat infants,
Killing pregnant mama rats for kicks,
And the rats that hadn't run crazy yet
Were in what you could call a fix.

Their red eyes swiveled, shot with The Fear,
But the fear just made them slow;
They clambered up the metal ladders
Toward the noplace their was to go,

Because now the flood was flicking toward
The bottom of the main deck slats,
And you couldn't tell the flood of the flood
From the blood of the flood of rats.

So it's only the few, worst rats survive,
While the meek take their final dip.
Just the worst rats left to save themselves
On another sinking ship.

The Four Geese Dance

Four geese, appearing lost but of course not
Lost, came barking out of the western afterglow,
Improbable long necks arrowing toward a spot
Their tiny brains could scarcely think, only know.

I turned toward their first sounding, then slowly wheeled
To follow the veering arrowhead of their flight,
Craning my neck as my feet turned on the winter field
Of grass and weed until they were clean out of sight.

I could only see the little half-circle I could see.
The geese could see their unseen flock, rowing
Toward the unseen lake they'd sleep on. Me -
I could merely understand how far understanding lies from
knowing.

The Miller Moths

It's a hot year
And it was a warm winter.
The millers are out in thousands,

Disturbing the twilight.
Their flight is gibberish,
Like television with the sound off.

They fly with desperate intensity
But no sense of direction,
Bashing into solids until they

Trap themselves behind a window blind
And bat their lives away.
Grey as true death,

Intense and insane as real life,
Two purposes only:
Survive long enough to reproduce,

And pollinate the yucca flowers,
Those phosphorescent candles
Whose light stays on the hillside

Even after true night falls.

Secret

Three times divorced,
minimally employed,
driving a broken car

among idiot drivers
whose own cars cost more
than my shotgun house is worth,

my talents unwanted,
my learning obsolete...
my windshield wipers

give up the ghost
without prior warning.
Sure, I think. Why not?

I abandon the car,
slog through the piling snow
to the daycare house.

I look through the window
at you playing happily
with strangers. Knock.

We hug silently.
Say goodnight.
Walk home laughing in the snow.

Uncle Milton's Giant Ant Farm

The ants came in yesterday's mail,
thirty or so in a plastic tube
brown with formic acid.

We let them trapeze out of the tube,
dropping down into
Uncle Milton's Giant Ant Farm.
They set to work immediately,
as advertised. By the time
we returned from watching the Cubs
take the Pirates in eleven
on the cable at Bill's house,
tunnels and caves were well started.

Tonight, they'd hauled up mountains,
white crumbs of sand
grain by grain, and the tunnels snaked
everywhere. A couple of ants
were balled up in death.
The one you named Michelle
carried one of them in her jaws
over the green plastic bridge
and lay him down on the highest hill.
We watched them as we ate
mostaciolli and cheese and carrots,

talking about why some had died.

At the library, Patches the Guinea Pig
was still there, still alive and munching,
and we found two books about Lincoln,
and I found a new Bill Granger.
It was cool walking back to the car,
a big sky blowing over St. Mary's steeple.

You brushed your teeth,
we got started on the first Lincoln book,
I locked the kitten in the bathroom
so she wouldn't keep you awake

purring in your face. The constituents
of great happiness are small
and fragile and they never stop moving,
not the whole night through.

The Nineties

Watch the News

A many-tonned object full of humans
fell out of the sky today.

Today the wind blew while rain fell
out of the sky.

These events fascinated those who tell
what happened.

Today those events were yesterday's,
but those who tell remain fascinated.

The utterly predictable, it seems,
comforts and fascinates everyone.

Watch the Sports

Tonight a famous home run hitter
hit a home run, his dunkty-oompth.

Tonight another famous home run hitter
failed to hit his extieth.

These facts fascinated those who bring news
and those who receive news.

The News for Sports

Watching the famous plane wreck,
Cal considered his front door,

which he'd just shattered in response
to his failure to succeed in his wife's eyes.

Tonight the famous home run hitter had hit a ball
so hard on the ground
that the shortstop couldn't reach it
and the winning run scored.

And many, many were going insane
on this Friday night,

they were driving their cars into bridges,
provoking their lovers to fight,

throwing their children into walls,
they were thinking they were right.

They were not famous, nor had they won
the game, nor had they colorfully lost

their lives. Nor had they any space left
within their brains in which to fashion

a new life with the nothing of them
left in there that remained.

Watch the Weather

The weather today was as Cal experienced it.
No matter. As calf to tit,

Cal waits through message after message
from companies that despise him

to see what tomorrow will bring in the way of weather. He intends to be prepared.

Muscular Christians

How many, hungover and unkempt,
surly with Saturday, have you flushed
from their sweating beds,
with your crude pulp paper texts
in hand, always in pairs,
polite, unmemorable faces
scrubbed and shaven
pure as the faces of adolescent
mass murderers or model builders?

We cannot connect.
You read your poetry
serenely certain it is truth,
as if when you hungered
a recipe would suffice.
None of my money
for your god who never laughs,
who makes offers
which cannot be refused,
like a mobster sending valentines.
I have seen what the literal do
when encouraged by numbers
in the icy persuasion
that their poetry, unlike
this sweating world, is true.

Still To Whisper Her Name
(for Dick Conway)

Her pale lynx eyes,
her short, full, ash-blonde mane,
high Slavic cheekbones
and her bare arm I can see today,
as I can see myself,
sixteen, pimpled, lower class,
walking the dark sidewalks
of her neighborhood,
beneath the arched vault
of elms and oaks,
a long gallery of lighted windows
and her concealed somewhere
within the white, green-shuttered dormer,
untouchable and perfect
as I walk yearning
on through the pollened night.

Fats Waller

I present you with a disgusting floor,
covered with ocher lumps of puke,
piles of paper refuse, cigarette butts,
all swimming in a sea of black water.

Can you remove this human nasty?
Of course you can!
Just let me sit down on this bench,
touch my tips to the keys.

Look and listen: the Great God
is in the air, breathing.
Put your tip to whatever it want to touch.
Feel what come back.

Go on, now, you - Go On!
What do you see? The world
clean as when born,
and the birds asleep sing.

The Theatre

The questions
so rarely present themselves
in the fashion of drama,
self-proclaimed.

They merely surround,
like the air
and the unnoticed birds
in the invisible trees.

The moments of decision
are rare as black rhinos
for most human lives,
and when they arrive,

they arrive like death,
with another breakfast.
The drama
is a million instants long,

and what heroes exist
make many small choices.
To withhold cruelty.
To hope, again.

To love what always vanishes.

The Stare of the Dying
(for Richard and Sophie)

The dying stare beyond you
into some other world
when you look into their eyes.

They gaze intently
beyond your care, your grief,
beyond your dream.

Tonight, you stare up toward
where my friend sang his last song,
silenced as he was.

He'd been gone a day,
and where you look now, a bird sang,
wild and lovely as a meadowlark.

Our grieving is so hard,
even when we know it foolish
and selfish. We want to go with,

To that place you see with placid,
waiting eyes. We want to join you
where death can't unjoin us ever again.

The 20th Century Limited

Ma and Pa overall bibbed
and tuckered in a hundred little towns
hurl past the windows
and the fields between
wheel ochre rows of cornstalks
turning fawn and fractured
cast with white
past the window and the platforms
escape past the window
you get the idea
the train isn't moving at all
the tracks were never laid
all those chinamen and slaves
and Lincolns and Chevrolets
and gaslit carnivals, beach-togged
striplings, Ferris-wheel rapes,
boys slung with catfish,
Polack tenements, Victory Gardens,
tomatoes strapped to stakes
were part of the diorama
winding past the window
accelerando, though, always
accelerando, which is why
I keep dashing out of my sleeper
to the same Western Union

stop after stop
where old snotshirt dozes
and wake him up
ruder and ruder
to send telegram
concerning present location
of train which
stop
is always
stop
the same.

Our Big Brains

"But now her own big brain was urging her to take the polyethylene garment bag from around a red evening dress in her closet there in Guayaquil, and to wrap it around her head, thus depriving her cells of oxygen." - Kurt Vonnegut, Galapagos

The truth is,
I'll never have time
to completely appreciate one
of the hundreds of great musicians
who've saved and enriched me,
from Handel to Paolo Conte,
or to assist one other person
to hear the little I have heard.

No one has time
to hear all that's to be heard
to see what's to be seen
smell what's to be smelt
taste all the tastes or
feel what each second should be felt.

The truth is,
every damn one of us
is nothing but a little amoeba
with legs and arms and thumbs
and a great big brain,
circling around a random pebble
on the deep bottom of a great ocean,

while up on land Triceratops plows along,
sublimely unaware
of our piddling existence.

The truth is,
the truth is bigger than Triceratops,
bigger than the oceans ten times
ten times themselves,
bigger than 8 turned sideways.

The truth is,
not one of us, get busy as busy
we can, can ever know
what the truth is.

Are you humbled yet? Are you humbled yet?

The Prairie Dogs

Here are the borders: North, a four-lane highway;
South, an access road that leads to East, a parking lot.
West, a residential street. You may live within these,
within half a city block left accidentally unimproved.

Enough. You can burrow, construct a colony,
find food enough above. What more do you need?
Food, shelter, enough water, a sort of air.
Who could ask for anything more?

Who could ask for anything more
than to rise up into the day trembling with fear,
and to venture out fearfully onto one's front porch,
looking always three hundred sixty degrees

around and one hundred eighty above?
And, showered with blessings, find
no predator within range?
Then, one can begin to live -

to snake over the ground, finding
seeds to snatch and -
first checking, first checking all the terrible
roundness - stuff in one's cheeks?

Then, when one sees one's fellows

out all over the great, buff field
stuffing and snaking,
to feel that everything is as it should be?

Perhaps you only rear like a pony
out of habit then, but if you do,
others will rear too,
and half the colony will run back

and disappear into their homes.
If a kite lands sudden as death from nowhere,
fleering his blueblack scissortail
to set his balance on earth,

you'll all disappear underground.
You do your part of the world's old work,
and who am I to despise your caution?
I ask this from my burrow, you dogs.

The Snout Beetles

For years now the hollyhocks
Have done poorly,
Their buds sucked by snout beetles.

All through June
The snout beetles work
On the early buds,

Sucking much life
Out of the whole shebang:
Buds, leaves, stalks.

They drive their wedge heads
Into the buds
Until the buds go pale yellow.

While one sucks the bud,
Another mounts it from behind.
Battleship grey, they look

Like pygmy rhinos humping.
Their sonar detects a watcher
And they disappear

Under the crenellations of the buds.

Only poison discourages them,
But I think they just retreat

To the bottom stalks,
Lay eggs for next year.
And the poison doesn't stop.

"They just eat and screw,"
Elaine says; "That's the worst of it."
That is the worst of it.

The Chain of Cashel

Behind the motel where I will sleep tonight,
flanked by the ceaseless, dull doppler of two highways,
a small swale cradles a stagnant pond,
brackish and mud-brown in the pewter evening,
edged by a mess of winter-wheatened cattails.

On their shaggy, balding crowns, three dozen
red winged blackbirds rest, easily
balanced on the yard-high stalks,
and in the acid rain of tires sing.

With what variety - long rattles, as from fat,
feathered crickets; brief chirks like finches',
but more authoritative; two-note melodic phrases.
A long, communal concerto, discussing
territories, mates, and who knows what else.

Every minute or so, another blackbird appears
from the grey clouds, wheels with impossible economy
down to a perfect, bounceless landing
on a barely budded twig in the poplar that stands
above the swale, and there joins an intricate dance
from higher twig to lower and around again -
all this with no air traffic controller
tense at the mike before his glowing green screen.

The blackbirds in the cattails keep the music
going for the dance, seldom moving unless to rise
into a tight circle and return to the original perch,
as a trumpeter might shift to surreptitiously
shake his spit valve clean.

No. Not a concerto, not a sonata,
no beginning - middle - end business -
not even a suite, even if it does
accompany a set of dances. These red winged blackbirds,
truer black than ravens, and that black
blacker yet in the yellow-bordered scarlet
light the slashes on their epaulets provide,
these red winged blackbirds sing about
no human dance, sing in no human form.

If I were less agnostic, I would say they sing
the song of God, the circle song,
whose beginning swallows its end
like the chain of Cashel.
I will say that anyway.

Crow

This black is not the absence
of light, not this crow's,
no, sir, no more than love
a dearth of hate or courage
of fear. Look:
they convivify
on the green park grass,
snapping curious heads
at squirrels disemboldened
by their stares,
at bug rustles, at cellophane,
at any of the passing parade.

Look how they twitch ass,
paw air with deliberate claws,
enjoy the morning, enjoy
the afternoon, good
evening to you, sir.

Rise up singing harmony
that's not quite unison,
not quite question,
call, call, call each other,
independent until the answer:
rise up together, put shoulder

into wheel across the paling blue
to homes made of home,
stick-castles in the trees
where they are born,
where they will never die.

We All Want to Change the World

I took my daughter and her boyfriend to dinner
at a place called Joe's Crab Shack.
Strategically installed near the entrance
to the town's first shopping mall, Joe's
presented thousands of winking lights
that glanced off reproduced tin signs
promoting products unavailable
since the 50's, taped music of the Beatles
and the Bee Gees, fancifully named
seafood dishes, though we were far from the sea.
Teenaged waitresses and busboys
broke spontaneously into disco dances
when called upon by their contracts
to celebrate life. Inside this giant pinball
machine, I forgot what I had ordered
before I finished consuming it.
It was a family restaurant, calibrated
perfectly to our two generations:
my daughter's, for which the past
consists of strip-mined artifacts,
and mine, whose contribution
has been to further refine
the art of putting everything
up for sale.

We were far from the sea.

Alley Thoughts

Walking down the alley toward home,
whacking the dirt off my pants with dirty hands,
the dust joins the dust in the sunset,
Amos & Andy in the air, unmistakable voices
incomprehensible out here in the alley,
a tinny radio car crash, another crash,
the people laugh, hollyhocks dusted with laughter
and the dust in the air the late sun shines through:
The week is over.

I will not have to talk to the man for two days.
I will not have to talk to the woman for two days.
I will not have to correct my telescope for two days.
I will not have to not butter my bread for two days.

Walking down the alley toward home.
Mrs. Mellon's old lab rises up behind her fence
to bark at me, and I reach over the fence to scratch
behind her ears, her dusty coat so thin in the fence shadow.
She can't get her feet up on the fence as she used to,
anymore than Mrs. Mellon can tend to her back yard,
but she can still wriggle her stiffened spine
if I scratch the right spot.

I will not have to talk to the man for two days.
I will not have to talk to the woman for two days.
I will not have to pretend I didn't hear that for two days.
I will not have to set the clock for two days.

Above the alley two pearl-grey doves sit two feet apart,
one one wire down from the other,
the famous lovebirds, almost shadows against the shadow
evening sky
behind them, sitting and sitting,
not mourning, not singing, not making a sound or a move
for that matter; their heads don't even move as I walk by,
they're watching something I can't see.
The week is over.

I will not have to talk to the man for two days.
I probably will not talk to the woman for two days.
She probably will not talk to me for two days.
Though dust settles and doves do move.

Act

Late summer had toasted the grass and weeds,
But in the field I nevertheless found a dandelion ghost,
A perfectly spherical puffball of a hundred seeds.
I pinched it off and huffed and watched the seeds coast

On the random eddies, out, out from my breath
Over the exhausted field, like paratroops let from a plane
Descending on a placid country not expecting death
Or life to visit in such sudden, delicate rain.

And as I sent the sphere exploding to naught,
I realized my act had some supposed significance,
Something about love or wishes, but I'd forgot
What it was, and so it was nothing but a blind dance

On a dying field, which whether or not it needs
Them, will next Spring birth more flowers or pernicious
weeds.

Glory

Above the peaks, a meaningless cumulonimbus
splayed its parting parts, enclosing the late sun,
whose shafts erupted through the central tendrils,
lighting them silver too intense for word.

Two dark starlings skipped random as stones over water
into the darkness advertised by this glory.
A swarm of bull gnats clouded my head while the starlings
disappeared, and first I thought they danced in my eyes.

They swarm, I recently learned, to attract a female gnat,
who will choose one from their multitude.
When I focused again upon the departing sun,
whatever I had seen had changed beyond recall.

Seven-Fifteen P.M. on the Last Night of the Millenium

The crows were hanging out in one stand of bare elms
at the edge of the field, great slanted clots of black fruit
calling crow among themselves, once in a while rising up
like a film gone backward to settle on a different set
of winter-deadened trees, where they continued their
shenanigans, gang bangers mocking an old man
walking with his two old dogs, dogs who've given up
even pretending to chase crows, rising again to yet
another set of crowns to voice their utter scorn
for all poor civilized creatures who'll never get born.

The New Millennium

Working One's Way Through West's Colorado Digest
of 1998 Legal Decisions in the State of Colorado

Abandoned to Appeal and Error,

Crops to Divorce,

Divorce to Writs of Entry.

Forcible Entry to Hospitals.

Poisons to Receivers.

Steam to Trial.

Judgement to Larceny.

Equity to Execution.

Pardon and Parole to Pledges.

Four Dots and a Dash.... a Catalog of Books I Will Not Be Purchasing

1. Trusc 2 : The Mysterious Disappearance, by Nigel Smith

When Etruscan detective Aman "Trusc" Hovep is called to Nineveh to investigate the mysterious disappearance of a....

2. Out of Training: a Joye Jennifer Mystery, by Victoria Spenser

When perky but lethal personal trainer to the stars Joye Jennifer finds her nearing-the-A-list trainee Brad Carpathio hanged by his....

3. Wretchedness, by F.R. Usserenjaiz

In the autumn of his life, Gregor Zvzeanorgeu begins to discover that he is alone on an ice floe in the Bergen Straits owing to his own efforts that began the night he first heard Madame Guvina sing....

4. The Honey on the Horn, by P.S. Tinley

In the deep winter of 1752, a Siberian peasant dug up a fossilized reindeer antler encrusted with petrified honey. This discovery eventuated in the American Revolution, and Oxford University professor Dr. Tinley (yes, that Oxford) explains how a hunk of moribund honey inspired....

5. I'll Ralph Today, by Starr Starr

No holds are barred as the author, who some readers will recall, reveals her utterly unrewarding pursuit of nirvana along the paths of mindless fornication with anyone remotely associated with the media who might advance her career. Her disappointment jump starts her journey to....

6. What I Wiped Up on Tuesday, by I.B. Slaven

Winner of the Bollenball, Pullzanner and Sourelit Prizes, Ms Slaven has answered her honors with a new collection of poems that honor those who have honored her, and in the most honorable sense of the....

7. I Love Everybody But Blind People, by Joyce Goodkind

Joey's prejudice is revealed when his entire set of progenitors begins to stagger around leaning on canes and barking piteously. When Joey's eyes are opened, the illustrations become truly appalling, and Joey learns that....

8. Hope for a Troubled Millennium, edited by Lucinda Light

Victim of a Dickensian youth and a Dickensonian middle age, the editor has assembled here every tale ever told, from the shivering shadows of antediluvian caves to the equally sepulchral caves beneath our modern cities, where victims of international cartels die enmucked in silence, to reveal the hope that resides....

9. Four Rots and a Rash: My Illness in Great Detail, by Don Thompson Johnston

This courageous memoir recounts, from an apparently minute-by-minute journal, the progress of the author's multitudinous afflictions, from which he has yet to....

10. Poodles Are My Weakness, by Gorselyn Fairview

Did you ever really think about poodles? Gorselyn Fairview has, and....

Revoltin' Development

My kind falls short on compassion
for all the other kinds.
Chains and bob wire are in fashion
to make our ties that bind.

We think the other kinds are good
for slaves or pets.
We seldom feel inclined
to pay them any debts.

We pull their teeth with pliers,
teach them to kill for our fun,
factory them into friers,
shoot them before they can run.

Beat them like rented anythings,
Feed them poison pellets.
Rip out their claws and their stings.
Bash them to death with mallets.

We think our kind was created
to make use of creation,
our breath perpetually bated
to give ourselves an ovation.

Let's hear it for us, we say,
Kings of the firmament.
Looks to us that our day
of preeminence is permanent.

The others we think our debtors
live with only this hope in mind:
We treat our kind no better
than we treat the other kind.

The Hawk Moth

I walk down the steps from my front door at dawn
expecting nothing but the newspaper,
but here are these flocks of daffodils glowing
like yellow lamps in strangers' windows
behind night's last smoke that wreathes
through the leafless branches of lilac and sumac,
smoke tasting sweet as the lightening air.

A hawk moth is working before my eyes,
still as a stamen in a daffodil's throat,
hovering steadier than a hummingbird,
her revving wings utterly soundless;
perfect, in short. A hawkmoth, translating
her motionless thorax and bowed abdomen
from one daffodil to the next
without apparent effort. Without moving, in fact.

About as colorful in this lifting dusk
as an old woman's beige wool sock,
she doesn't hover; she stands still;
until the plastic-wrapped Gazette whacks
the sidewalk, and she is gone.

Here's me, standing after sun-up,
one last glance at the daffodils before I turn
to the newspaper's awful chronicle of human failure
to see anything at all but itself ever any more.

The Crows Take Up Golfing

Four crows browse on the fairway,
stepping forward carefully,
as if waiting for another to play first,
though looking, in fact, to see

careless grubs or worms.
Another crow might beat the first
to one of them, if he didn't keep
his eyes peeled. That would be

such a pity.

Petit Guignol:
(On the news of my friend's Honorable Mention)

We are the damned,
accursed by faint praise,
familiar with the death
embedded in a measured phrase.

We bear the scars
of all ten thousand cuts
administered
by the Devils If and But.

We are the small print
life's eye prefers to skip,
coffined, hands folded
over one last rejection slip.

Honorable mention
dishonors all we submit.
Our only glory was
we never quit.

7 Innings for Kazuo Matsui

At the plate, his stance
so like Hideki's, but poised,
not clenched: in balance.

Before ball is hit,
He's heading for where it goes.
Complete attention.

His arm no cannon,
his throw is in the target,
zen archer's arrow.

His number seven
that of the greatly gifted
Mantle, child of gods.

He is no god's child,
merely a man who does with
his gifts what he can.

Eyes wide as child's eyes
should frighten any pitcher.
Some pitchers are fools.

Kazuo Matsui.
What all teams require to win:
happy warrior.

Dogs

To dispense with the obvious:
the way they smell in the house,
come in from the rain, mud
between their calloused pads,
happily flipping loose skinsfull
of drops shining in the sun
after you've washed the skunk
out of them, happily sniffing
privates, their own, your own,
anybody's own,
like talkshow hosts,
shameless, tasteless,
munching their own turds
and happy to do so, mounting
or being mounted as brainlessly
and unromantically as you ever did,
and, taken as a species,
the very definition of undignified.

Watching you every waking minute,
accepting your petty rage,
waiting for you to remember their thirst,
hoping you will scratch
the perfect place or any place or at all,
or remember they exist
in your home
so they can exercise forgiveness.

For I Will Consider My Cat Sylvia

Nearly every night
I roll slowly around on the floor,
studying to undo the hurt
I've done myself during the day,
not to mention the bad habits
learned early and deeply ingrained.

My cat Sylvia - using the word "my"
loosely - sometimes joins me.

She effortlessly becomes part of the carpet's skin.
She becomes a skeleton -
and you can't get more relaxed than that.

Lids at three-quarter mast,
she peers curiously at my labored contortions
as I work to achieve her natural state.

I can savor all this in my big brain,
and I do, to the detriment of my mission.

Meanwhile, Sylvia tolerates me:
"He's a good enough one of a damned bad lot.
About as slow a student as I've ever seen, but
he tries. He tries."

Roger Maris Reflects

"What would the New York writers say if they knew my uncle was Adolf Eichmann?"
- Roger Maris

Other day, while watching television
in a bar at noon in North Dakota,
I saw some ancient interview
where the guy asked me something
and I didn't answer but he did.

He didn't know what he was asking.
Wouldn't have understood any actual answer.
So I didn't say anything. Stayed mum.
The show had me either arrogant or dumb.

Now, the reason I was in a bar
that time of day was just I'd taken
one kid to his game and another
to a friend's house, and I had a little time to kill.
Know anything better
than beer and tv for that?
Bet you don't.

Controlled Touching

"...controlled touching ought to be permitted for registered blind persons only,
and only with the consent of the dancer."

Are it not protuberant, do it not protrude
that this right of controlled touching here
be limited to the less than sighted, whereas
the controlled touching perquisites not
to mention rights of all those insufficient
auditories, less than wholly ambulatories,
all those less confident, less gifted,
less well-endowed by ambition or brain -
not to mention, not to mention myriad
others mysteriously falling short -

My lawyer won't shut up.
I tug his coat, I hiss,
I kick him behind the knee.
He won't stop making demands.

What I want seems simple
enough, can't be demanded:
uncontrolled touching.
No guards, no peepers,

no latex, no social safety
nets and snares. Touching.

Just let me touch her,
and if consent meet consent,

let her touch me,
and as we touch each other,
consent and all the lawyers
swirl, founder, disappear.

The Last Vacant Lot in America

For nine years I've taken myself and my dogs,
now old, to the last vacant lot in America,
a half acre left alone, officially a grade school
playground. For me, a sacred place,
a field where nothing useful grows but grass
and weeds and a small grove of random trees
down in the corner above the creek,
brindle green and tan and khaki
as the rains come and go and come again,
but down in the grove, even in winter,
some spruce show green to blue.

Last night a fox slipped under the fence
along the creek bank and smoked
through the high grass. My dogs
are so old they didn't even notice her.

Tonight the engines of improvement had arrived.
They'd ripped off half the field's scalp;
Roots lay in the rowelled dirt like severed fingers.
They'd dozered back the edges of the grove
and left the shreds of the improved trees
stacked like hay mows in the field.

A new steel fence kept the surviving trees back.
The old steel fence along the street,
erected to keep cars apart from children and dogs,
had been extracted, as if its roots might contain gold.

The engines had been busy. Now they rested,
huge, unbestial shapes in primary
yellow, red and blue, named for beasts
progress despises: caterpillar, deer, rhino.
They stood on the shadowed field
triumphant, madly sane and perfect,
as if M.C. Escher had come to visit.

A billboard in the school's front yard
and a line of young maples, planted as harbingers,
had proclaimed the advent of this progress.
All the maples had died of neglect since the board
went up. Architects' trees don't need care.

Sometimes the dogs and I would arrive
to find the whole field alive in crows,
bouncing and pecking and glowing black
in the dusk, and the dogs would leap
from the car and scatter them, scrawing,
into the oncoming night. Then the dogs
would come running back to me proud and slobbering.

The crows will still come,
and the foxes may, and geese will fly
over the playground perfect as the picture,
in which no children play.

Ode to Velveeta

I

I've heard you sneering,
snickering, deploring,
oh, yes. I'm sure no one
employed by NPR eats Velveeta.

Equally sure not one of them
has ever read the Velveeta label
or investigated the contents
of their preferred fromage.

But I don't want to talk
chemistry. I'm here
to talk Velveeta.
Velveeta: poetry. Vell -Veee - ta.

I tried to name my daughter
after it, but her mother
demurred. We named her
after Thelonious Monk instead.

II

In the second year
of the Korean War,
the one that's never ended,
only moved around,

I was the star left fielder
for my cub scout team,
The Rams. I was
also the only left fielder.

Before our night games,
my mother would cook me up
a mound of corned beef hash,
topped with melted Velveeta,

the late sun making a halo
of her fine hair, turning the kitchen
golden, the Cubs' Bert Wilson
calling the game on the radio.

She fried the hash crisp first,
then formed it into a mountain
and baked it until the orange cheese
cascaded down its slopes

over the crisp potato scree.
I ate it all and rose, fulfilled,
to go and be a hero
like Andy Pafko.

The Rams were a very bad

baseball team. We lost
one game 37 - 0,
called on account of darkness

before the top of the first had
ended. We never got to bat.
Not even Velveeta could
help us, that awful night.

Truth to tell, I wasn't
very good either,
and next year my eyes went bad.
So much for Andy Pafko.

III

Through all that's changed
and all that's not since then,
Velveeta has remained,
my friend, my comforter

in times of loss,
fellow celebrant
of the rare and fleeting win.
You can count on Velveeta.

In all those years
since I left left field to my betters,

Velveeta has never
been improved.

My cells have replaced themselves
nine times,
through all that's changed
and all that's not.

I'm 90% pure Velveeta now.
Might be, given ten more years,
a hero could still be born.
We could use a few.

Jayne Mansfield

I think we were eleven
that winter it never stopped snowing.
Old enough, anyhow, that when we set to rolling up boulders
of the heavy, wet stuff,
we began to see in the three classic, stacked globes
something new, something waiting to be revealed,
something that would not require buttons or a top hat.

We set to work then, sculpting
with our soaking, frozen gloves
under the vault of black oak limbs and branches,
and a frenzy came on us,
a hilarity that nullifed the cold and coming dark.

We were temporarily safe at school next day
when my mother discovered our creation,
a heroic statue of Jayne Mansfield,
celebrating her most celebrated attributes,
standing among the snow-plastered trees on our parkway,
gleaming in the early sun brilliant as alabaster.

When we got home that afternoon,
we found Jayne Mansfield reduced to snow chunks.
Only her foundation remained, disbodied, pillaged -
they had pillaged her, ruined her,
    knocked her to pieces.

My mother had done it with a broom, I heard later.
She said we were not ready for such things.
I see now she was right,
but those who wait until they're ready
quite often die before they even start.

Mourning Dove

A softly mourning dove
materialized to drink from the fountain
on the terrace where I worked,
resetting root-heaved flagstones.

I stopped, stooped, my head raised
to watch her drink and hear
the water splash itself.
I must have moved or made a sound,

and she was airborne, wheeling,
gone, only the sound her wings
made left behind. The sound
a playing card made in the spokes

of the black and red Schwinn
my Dad bought me. You fixed the card
to the back fender strut with wire,
bent it in, and off you went,

making a rising whirr, almost as if
you had a motorbike beneath you.
I went back to my work, wondering
where my time had gotten to.

Second Ending

When all the starlings, robins, jays
Have given up and gone to nest,
The crows refuse the calling night,
Defer the final rest.

Over the waiting conifers,
They improvise an arabesque,
A final celebration
To the dying fire in the West.

Like fighter pilots when flight was new,
Over the field they chase and dive,
Rise like ash from an unseen fire,
Circle like everything alive.

The second ending, it's called in jazz,
Refuse to let go and get gone:
One more once, Count Basie says,
Let the song sing its love of the song.

Round Lake

One year of my life, I fished Round Lake.
No fish lived in it, but it was still alive.
No one else fished it; it was reputed dead.
No one had faith but me,

And I had none either. I knew
I'd never feel a tug all year.
Each time I'd rent the only rowboat left
from the dying man in the dying shack,

and row out slowly to where fish would be,
pike, maybe, along the reed bed edges
where the water looked like amber tea,
and my Daredevil swiveled

like a victor's flag through liberated crowds
of waving, slime-feathered bottom weeds,
and came up empty every time.
There were no fish in that lake.

I'd sit on the rowboat's aft seat,
listen to cicadas grinding in the pines,
watch the midges dance to their tune,
and be alone and glad of it.

One time, rowing in, I heard a flop
only a fish could make resound
and Round Lake turned topaz in the sunset,
and that's all I know about love.

www.ingramcontent.com/pod-product-compliance
Lightning Source LLC
Chambersburg PA
CBHW020859090426
42736CB00008B/435
9780984413942